The Babysitter's Guide

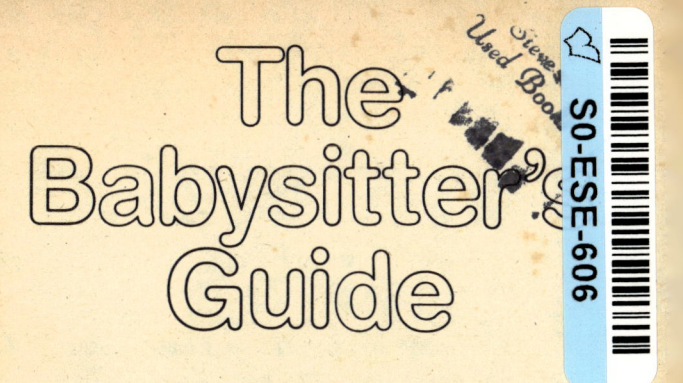

Sharon Sherman

**with cartoons by
Mark Lasky**

SCHOLASTIC BOOK SERVICES
New York Toronto London Auckland Sydney Tokyo

No part of this publication may be reproduced in whole or in part, or stored in a retrieval system, or transmitted in any form or by any means, electronic, mechanical, photocopying, recording, or otherwise, without written permission of the publisher. For information regarding permission, write to Scholastic Book Services, 50 West 44th Street, New York, New York 10036.

ISBN 0-590-31342-8

Copyright © Scholastic Magazines, Inc., 1969, 1979. All rights reserved. Published by Scholastic Book Services, a Division of Scholastic Magazines, Inc.

12 11 10 9 8 7 6 5 4 3 2 1   12   9/7 0 1 2 3 4/8

Printed in the U. S. A.   06

Contents

Introduction v
1. The Business of Babysitting 1
2. You and the Children You Know 9
3. Clues for Child Care 15
4. Sitter's Guide to Safety 33
5. Building In Good Behavior 39
6. The Magic of Play 47
7. About Books for Children 56
8. Babysitting as Big Business 63
9. What Every Babysitter Should Know 75

Introduction

Why be a babysitter?

Probably for the same reason one friend is a stock boy at a local grocery store and another works part-time in a department store.

You want to earn money.

But babysitting is not just a business. Even though you get paid for it, it is a very real service to parents. With your help they can take part in adult activities they might otherwise miss. They can have an occasional "rest" from child care which will make them better parents.

Since service is a two-way street, you'll gain some things from babysitting too—in addition to the money you earn.

You'll get experience in dealing with people outside your family and school groups. You'll see the different ways people approach marriage and child-rearing. And, watching children, you'll get some interesting insights into your own behavior.

Of course, what you get out of babysitting— whether in terms of money or experience — depends on how much you put into it.

This book will help you get the most out of babysitting. As you will see, only two chapters are given to the business side of this part-time job. We know you'll make money by babysitting. We hope our "nonbusiness" chapters will help you get the more valuable return — experience.

O·N·E

The Business of Babysitting

Going into any business involves an investment, and babysitting is no exception. Your initial investment will be time spent in getting the word around that you're willing to be a "substitute parent."

Talk to friends who are already in the babysitting business. Ask them to recommend you when they're unable to take a job.

Ask your mother to let her friends know you're in business. If they don't have small children, the chances are they know people who do.

Keep your ears open when you're doing errands in local stores. Many of your jobs may start with a chance remark from a mother that she "just can't find a babysitter for tonight."

While you're advertising your willingness to babysit, be learning what is expected of you and what to expect of your clients.

Find out what most of your town's babysitters charge for their services. For most small towns and cities, the going rate is between $.75 and $1.50 an hour for basic babysitting chores. In cities where babysitters often take buses or trains to their jobs, the price may be as high as $2.00 or more. Most girls charge extra for sitting with more than one child. For each additional child, they usually add $.50 or more to the basic hourly rate.

Decide what you'll charge before your first job offer—then let your customers know what the cost will be before you accept the job.

Also remember to ask how many hours you will be expected to work and whether or not the family will provide transportation to and from their house.

Once you have accepted a job, you have an obligation to be there. Avoid last minute chores, telephone calls, or delays. When people are planning an evening out it is inconsiderate and wrong to disappoint them, unless, of course, an emergency or illness forces you to cancel. Don't decide you'd rather see a movie that night unless you can find someone to take over your babysitting job. Any such changes will have to be approved by your customer ahead of time, of course.

At some time a really important conflict will occur. If you value your business reputation, you'll give your customers as much notice as possible when you must cancel a job. And you'll do your best to help them find another sitter for the job.

If a customer doesn't know you personally, she may ask you to visit her ahead of time and meet the children, or to come early on the night you'll be working. This is probably something you should suggest if your employer doesn't think of it. It will give you the opportunity to meet the children, see how they behave with their parents and strangers, and offer you a chance to become familiar with the house you will be sitting in. This opportunity may also be your lucky chance to have "second thoughts" about babysitting—or babysitting for this particular job! Another consideration for babysitters is how to talk to the parents. Some parents may want to hire a babysitter but may be very fearful about allowing anyone else the responsibility to care for their child. A parent may be nervous about leaving and you can do many things to make the separation easier.

a. Act confident...because you really are! Be prepared for last-minute tears from the child you are sitting for. Try to reassure the parents — you're used to tears...it really does happen quite frequently with young children. Also be prepared for last-minute worries and instructions from your employer.

b. Be prepared to distract a child who is upset because the parent is leaving. If you have not met the child before the time of your job think about the possibilities of temper tantrums, tears, and fears about parents leaving. Decide what you will do *before* it happens!

SOME BASIC QUESTIONS
What will your job involve?

If you're sitting with an infant, he will probably be asleep when you arrive. Ask the mother to show you where diapers and other supplies are kept. During the evening, check about every half hour to see that the baby is dry and well covered. Most small babies won't wake at all — which leaves you free to study or watch TV. But remember that the child, not entertainment, is your reason for being there.

If you're sitting with an older child, find out whether you're supposed to feed him. If you are, the mother should tell you what food to give him and explain his usual mealtime routine. Ask her about snacks, too, because he's sure to try raiding the cookie jar as soon as Mommy is gone.

Where can parents—or other adults— be reached in an emergency?

When parents walk out the door, you're on your own, and the responsibility for the safety of the children and the house is yours. Be professional about your job. Don't call friends on the telephone or invite them to come over. Have a snack or watch TV only if you have been invited to do so by your customer.

Teenagers who take their babysitting jobs seriously rarely have trouble finding work. So hang your appointment book by the family phone and open a savings account — you're in business.

Before the parents leave, you should have a telephone number for the parents, the family doctor, the police and fire departments, and a competent neighbor. Many teens use forms like the one on the next page to record such information.

In the back of this book, you will find additional copies of the "For My Information" sheet which you can cut out and use for your different clients. They will then become a handy reference, along with the other information in this book.

(P.S. Some teenagers have turned babysitting into business on a grand scale. See the last chapter in this book for some exciting ideas you might want to try.)

For My Information

PHONE NUMBERS:

Parents _____

Relative _____

Neighbor _____

Doctor _____

Fire Department — Dial Operator and ask for Fire Department.

Police — Dial Operator, ask for police.

EQUIPMENT:

Diapers, bedclothes, blankets _____

_____

First-Aid Kit _____

INSTRUCTIONS FOR FEEDING:

Time _____

Menu and where to find food _____

_____

Range (how to light) _____

INSTRUCTIONS FOR BEDTIME:

Time _____ Bath _____

Snack _____ Ventilation _____

TIME PARENTS ARE EXPECTED BACK

_____

T·W·O

You and the Children You Know

You probably know many children of all ages—relatives, younger brothers or sisters, or neighbors down the street. Perhaps you have never paid them much attention unless they demanded it or ever bothered to analyze why they did or said a particular thing. Babysitting will give you a good chance to observe children in ways you never have before.

Watch them closely and you'll learn, not only about them, but about yourself.

Each of us can learn from a child, says Katherine Read in *The Nursery School: A Human Relations Laboratory* (Saunders), because we all have these things in common:

We were all children once.

We are all members of families.

We all met some frustration in growing up.

We all tend to resist change.

We all have feelings that need draining off.

As you watch a child learn to control his own emotions and to interact well with others, you'll understand better some of your own "growing pains."

Here are a few guidelines for dealing with children of any age:

Observe children of the same age and notice the differences among them. You'll see that no two children grow at the same rate. You'll also notice that a child may be older in some ways than he is in others. Johnny may climb better than most children his age, but be slower than others in talking.

Have some idea what a child might be like at each age level, but don't expect any child to fit all parts of the pattern. (Chapter 3 gives some characteristics of the "average" child at different ages. Use it as a framework for the things you'll learn about individual children.)

Think about what may be behind a child's actions. You may not understand the reason, but there is a reason behind everything a child does. If you ask Alan why he hit Richard, he'll probably say, "Because he hit me first," "Because I don't like him," or "I don't know. I just felt like hitting."

Before you scold or punish, try to hear not only what his words say, but what's beneath them: "I don't know what to do when I'm angry," "I'm afraid that you love Richard more than me," or "There's something else bothering me and I don't know how to tell you."

It's amazing how fast most children learn good behavior when adults discover the real reasons for their misbehavior.

Allow a child to experiment. He'll love learning that he can turn a handle and make water come out of a pipe, or push a button and make lights go on in a dark room. As long as he isn't likely to hurt himself or others, let him try. Keep in mind that you are only a babysitter! By this, I mean that it may make your job more interesting to involve yourself with "teaching," but don't expect to accomplish major changes in the personality or skills of the child for whom you are babysitting.

Provide appropriate equipment and materials for a child to use in play. Here's where the "age-achievement" guides can help. They tell you what physical abilities a child is likely to have at a certain age and what kinds of materials he can usually handle.

Answer a child's questions. Sally has a lot to learn and she learns a lot by asking. Give a simple explanation if you know the answer. If you don't, say so and offer to help find it in a book.

Give a child the responsibility of small tasks that are within his skill. But make sure the job is something that really needs to be done. Most children can sense when they've been given some unnecessary task just to get them out of the way.

Encourage a child, without pushing, to try new things when he's ready. Show that you love him (although you don't have to love everything he does).

Remember this guide for success in understanding children:

Every man is in certain respects
>   like all other men
>   like some other men
>   like no other man.*

*From *An Introduction to Child Study*, Ruth Strang (Macmillan).

T·H·R·E·E

Clues for Child Care

Infants

Soft skin and the smell of talcum powder, gurgles and coos, tiny fingers grasping your thumb—the appeal of a tiny infant is hard for most of us to resist.

But the prospect of being alone with a baby, and responsible for it, is enough to frighten any babysitter who hasn't had much experience with very small children. Before attempting to care for an infant be sure you know what you're getting into. Babies are fragile! It might be a good idea to set up a "practice session" before you accept the job of caring for an infant.

Caring for a baby *is* a big responsibility, but it needn't be frightening if you learn a few things about infants ahead of time.

An infant's basic physical needs are for food, warmth, cleanliness, sleep, and exercise.

Proper food for the baby must be determined by the doctor. Basically, the infant's diet will include milk (either his mother's or a prescribed formula), vitamin supplements, and water. Solid foods will be added as the doctor suggests.

Warmth and cleanliness are especially important because a baby has not built up an immunity to common germs, and because his skin is easily irritated. Even in hot weather, most newborn babies need a light cotton shirt.

Warmth is essential at bathtime, too. Until a baby is four to six weeks old, his body is extremely sensitive to varying temperatures, and it is best not to uncover him entirely. Sponge baths are adequate during this time. Before giving a baby a tub bath, watch someone else or practice under the supervision of an experienced person. The primary rule is never to take your eyes off the baby.

Sleep takes up the largest part of a newborn baby's life. After the first few weeks, he will wake at regular intervals for feeding. Otherwise, he rarely wakes unless he is uncomfortable. A very young infant sleeps in a curled position and usually doesn't move much. It's wise to vary the manner in which he is placed on the bed. Because his bones are soft, continually lying in one position may cause slight misshaping of his head.

Exercise helps a baby grow stronger. He will alternately relax and stiffen his body and will wave his arms and legs around. When an infant cries even though he is fed, dry, and apparently comfortable, his outbursts are usually a normal exercise of his lungs and vocal cords.

Every infant has a basic emotional need for love and security.

Love is felt in the warmth of your voice, the gentleness of your touch, the tenderness in the way you cuddle a baby. He will sense your irritation and anger, too, and he won't know that they're directed at yourself or others, not at him. Therefore, try to control your moods, particularly if you're not feeling as cheerful as you might.

Security is centered in the person who insures the baby's comfort. A baby likes routine and order. He won't worry when left alone if someone is there when he needs attention.

Every infant has natural instincts which govern his early behavior.

Inherent emotions, present at birth, are fear and curiosity. Since a baby has a natural fear of falling, always be sure he is supported. His fear of loud noises will lessen as he gets used to normal everyday sounds.

Curiosity helps the infant learn about his world by looking and touching. Popping objects into his mouth is a natural, if troublesome, habit. A baby's own body is particularly interesting to him — first as a part of his surroundings, then as something which belongs to him and which he can control.

Recognition of people as different from objects is the beginning of social behavior. Babies are not born social creatures, but they soon learn to enjoy contact with others. At about six weeks, an infant begins to recognize his mother or other persons most often with him. Distinguishing one person from another is usually possible by the fifth or sixth month.

Once he knows you, a baby will be happy to have you near him. And when you learn to understand and care for him, you can relax and enjoy him more.

A baby's limited physical ability changes gradually.

Proportions make an infant top-heavy. His head is too large for the rest of his body and usually bigger around than his chest. For this reason, his back and head must be well supported whenever he is held.

Infant muscular ability is limited to general movements. He cannot direct his limbs to touch any particular spot or object. Trying to teach him coordination is useless, for it will come naturally when his body is properly developed.

Growth has no set pattern. The normal sequence of grasping, reaching, sitting, crawling, and walking will take place when the child is physically and emotionally ready.

Special tips for sitting with an infant:

If all your skill can't calm a crying baby give him about 15 minutes to try to quiet himself. If he becomes ragingly red in the face or feels feverish, call his mother. And always call the mother, or a doctor, if the baby shows symptoms of illness, such as vomiting, coughing, difficulty in breathing, or the beginnings of a rash. Mothers would rather have a sitter over-cautious than under-cautious.

At bedtime speak softly or sing to soothe a baby who just can't settle down. Then place his favorite toy in bed with him.

Since the majority of babies sleep on their stomachs, place him gently on his tummy, turning his head to the side. If he seems fretful this way, you might turn him over on his back. Remove all pillows and loose blankets from the crib, check for drafts from open windows, and make sure the sides of the crib are locked up.

If he whimpers a bit, try not to go to him since he's obviously not too distressed. But if he really howls, delay his bedtime until he's sleepy enough not to be able to resist. Once he has surrendered to sleep, check him on the half hour to make sure he hasn't pulled the blankets over his head, and that he's comfortable.

Toddlers

"Toddlerhood" is that period in a child's life from about one-and-one-half to three years, from the time the baby is beginning to walk, or toddle, until he is quite steady on his legs. Because he can propel himself about, and has learned a new skill, he is eager to attempt others (such as tackling a set of stairs by himself), which means that you must keep up with him every minute.

As daring as an Arctic explorer, as nimble as the fastest magician, as exciting as a three-ring circus—that's a toddler. Although you may do homework or watch TV while babysitting, when it comes to toddler-tending, you've got to have your eye on your tiny charge constantly.

For, rest assured, if there's a ladder about, he'll climb it; if there's a button about, he'll taste it. But also rest assured, there's no fun or satisfaction equal to that of taking care of a two-year-old runabout full of curiosity and affection.

Because the toddler is growing out of babyhood, he is entering a new world which holds threats and confusions. Thunder, a siren, dogs, bicycles, even strange faces can terrify him, for they are new objects whose ability to hurt or give pleasure has not yet been tested. So many things are new to him that he needs the assurance of familiar objects and ways of doing things. It's up to you to offer warmth and affection so the child will feel secure.

How do you do this? Speak to him calmly, pleasantly, and quietly. Make his favorite toy available and don't expect him to share his toys with a sibling, for the toddler has not yet learned to share his belongings. If he's unreceptive to eating, to washing his hands and face before bed, to making a trip to the bathroom, don't force him to do these things. (But, if these problems arise more than two or three times, be sure to let the child's mother know.)

A toddler loves to pull, push, open, close, play hide-and-seek, play with water, blocks, sand, pots and pans, dolls, bright things, and soft things. At this age, objects often are popped right into the child's mouth, partly because he wants to "explore" them, sometimes because he is teething and needs something to chew on. If he wants to push a chair across the kitchen floor, let him (under your supervision);

if he wants to splash in the bathroom basin, encourage him.

Most of all, do try to enjoy his antics! A toddler can be a most entertaining creature. Try to grant the child's requests, within reason of course. You know how frustrated you would be if someone kept preventing you from doing a series of harmless things. The toddler feels exactly the same way, except that he will show his frustration while you would control yours.

How does the toddler show frustration? Perhaps, unintentionally, by bedwetting or a nightmare. Perhaps by disobedience or a tantrum. If a child you're minding has a tantrum, try to distract his attention. If you've just taken a dangerous object away from him, and he wants it, give him another equally desirable, but harmless, toy. Begin to read him a favorite story, a special treat for toddlers. Call him to come see the "beautiful pictures" in a book — toddlers love looking at bright pictures. And be sure the child gets enough rest, if not sleep, so that exhaustion doesn't make him difficult.

If you've ever said, "I'm so tired I could cry," you'll know how a small child must feel.

Don't frustrate a child by ignoring him; show interest in what he says and does. Praise his efforts and let him carry out projects with a minimum of help. Be sympathetic about his bumps and bruises. Often a child cries because of his need for a sympathetic kiss or cuddling, rather than from physical pain or discomfort.

Children of this age often go through a "no" period, when they react negatively to everything you may suggest. If a child refuses to cooperate, you might go gently ahead with the activity anyway. Once it's begun, there's every chance the child's "no" may turn to "yes." His negative responses are often reactions to the frustrations a growing child is beginning to face.

Showing favoritism to a baby brother or sister, breaking a promise, being inconsistent in your own behavior and in what you will or won't allow the child to do, shaming or humiliating a child, will not only make him distrust you, but can also make him react against you.

Of course, the toddler's safety and comfort are uppermost in your mind. Since he's just learning to talk and understand, he knows what a firm "no" from you means. And it's often just what he wants to hear, for children want discipline just as they want affection and understanding.

While babysitting for a toddler, remember:

If the toddler's mother has begun or finished toilet training him, you'll want to take him for bathroom checks, especially before bedtime. It's not unusual for a toddler to wet his bed. Treat such incidents casually; simply change the child and the bed clothes.

Remain constantly alert on the job. The need to discover and explore may lead the child into dangerous adventure when he pokes into the oven, turns on a hot water faucet, or tries to cut with a sharp scissors.

Toddler-tending requires equipment. Make

sure that the child's parents leave you sufficient toys, blocks, paper, etc. The best way to keep a toddler out of trouble is to keep him constructively busy.

Also get a menu from the mother, if you're on a full-day schedule, or a list of permissible snacks if it's a short-term project. A hungry child is a cranky child.

Make friends with the child. This is really very easy. All it requires is that you play with him. No one is as responsive as a toddler. If you get down on the floor and build blocks with him, he'll adore you.

As important as being friendly is being firm. But that doesn't mean spanking or scolding or nagging all the time. How do you avoid so many "no's"? Try to sidestep a situation where the child is grabbing at your pocketbook or a fragile figurine, by placing it out of reach, by giving him a scrap pad he can scribble on and not a book he must handle with care.

If you must take away something a toddler shouldn't have, it's easier not to do it by force. He'll put up a good fight, we warn you. Instead, try to divert him. "Tommy, just look at this!" will almost always capture his attention, simply because everything is new and wonderful to him. At that point you deftly remove the disputed object.

Give the child ample opportunity to "do" for himself. He's struggling bravely for independence. Let him get into his sweater by himself, or climb onto the couch in his own clumsy way. If he gets too frustrated, you can lend a hand.

Allow him to work off energy—he has loads of it. But slow him down, as bedtime approaches, with "quiet games." This can be anything from blocks to crayons. (Taboo before bedtime are exciting television shows, rough games.)

Bedtime is a ritual for any child. Upon the advice of his parents, offer your toddler a bedtime snack of milk and cookies or bread and butter. Next have him go to the toilet and then have his hands and face washed, and his teeth brushed. Tuck him in with sufficient blankets, seeing that there's enough air—but no draft—in the room. He may want you to sing to him or to tell him a goodnight story. A kiss will send him off to dreamland.

It's easy if you know toddlers. There's no menace in Dennis if you just handle him right!

Preschoolers

Four-year-old Timmy wants to know why the moon doesn't shine during the day, where the earth ends, and how he fits into his skin.

"How Timmy can ask questions!" you groan. Without knowing it, you have discovered a universal characteristic of preschoolers — enormous curiosity.

Consider yourself lucky if you have the opportunity to work with and care for preschoolers. They will charm and baffle you with their exuberant spirits, endless comments, and changing emotions. They ask worldly questions but quickly become innocent babes as they crawl in for a nap, clutching a bedraggled teddy bear or frayed blanket.

Despite great differences between a three-year-old and a five-year-old, both are considered preschoolers. And both do have many characteristics in common.

Like Jack's beanstalk, preschoolers grow and grow.

The entire body matures while legs and arms begin to stretch rapidly. The body "catches up" to the head and shoulders, in proportion. Large muscles are better coordinated than finer muscles (leg muscles as compared to finger muscles). This is important to remember when you plan activities. A four-year-old can ride a tricycle or play on the slide for longer periods than he can color with crayons.

The nervous system of the child grows rapidly, and reflexes appear stronger and more accurate. As the child grows, he gains great skill in handling his body.

Preschoolers need discipline, praise, and consistency — all sugar-coated with love.

Firmness proves to the preschooler that you love him enough to care what he's up to. But always, when you discipline him, make sure he understands that it is his actions you disapprove of, not the child himself.

Praise and approval are necessary to the happiness of a child. Unearned praise may spoil him; approval, honest and fair, gives him the incentive to try new ideas.

The preschool child has a great desire to be

independent, to prove that he's "not a baby." You can help by giving him things to do on his own, such as dressing himself. If you make it easy—with large buttons and front openings—he'll do well enough to earn your honest praise.

Consistent treatment is especially important to the child. A preschooler learns many things about himself and the world, in a short period of time. He must know that what is right today will be right tomorrow. To shame, ridicule, or belittle a child destroys his self-confidence and self-respect.

Preschoolers learn to give and take, to share, and to take turns.

Play, important to children and adults, fascinates preschoolers. It becomes serious business with them; it depicts their way of finding out what the world is like and what they can do in it. They also find that other people are important and must be considered. Timmy learns that it is not acceptable to bite, kick, or hit when Johnny takes a toy. You explain that it's better to talk out angry feelings instead of taking them out by hurting the other person.

When play gets too exuberant (and it will because children must let off steam) suggest another activity, such as reading a book or putting together a puzzle.

Because play is serious to them, Timmy and his playmates will never tire of nonsense rhymes, colorful words said over and over, or the same game played hours on end. Songs and guessing games entrance these youngsters. They also love to work with paints or crayons and cut paper.

The imagination of the preschooler knows no bounds. A blanket draped over chairs soon becomes a rambling house; a row of cardboard boxes becomes a fast-moving train.

Preschoolers need special attention at bedtime.

At day's end, most children are wound up and in need of a calming activity. Read a book or sing a song to relax the little one before tucking him in for the night.

Weary bodies grow defenseless and fears appear. If Timmy requests that you leave the night light on, do so with understanding. His lively imagination can introduce all types of scary animals into a dark room!

For parent or babysitter, the why-and-try years are tiring, exasperating, worrisome — and wonderful. At no other time in his life does the child approach the world with such unbounded enthusiasm and curiosity. It's a great joy to be around to help a little one learn "where the sun sleeps," and "how that rooster knows what time to crow in the mornings."

In-Schoolers

Grade-school children challenge a babysitter.

Six- and seven-year-olds will be easier to care for and understand than eleven- or twelve-year-olds, who are nearer your own age. But you can win the preteen's confidence and gain acceptance if you remember how you felt at this age.

Keep in mind that "a child is more like himself than anyone else." Each child is different from every other — in growth, in feelings, and in action. He'll get where he's going at his own pace, developing those characteristics which make him a special individual.

From ages six to twelve, physical growth usually doubles the child's size and completely changes his appearance.

The youngest school children are just emerging from the preschool years. Their bodies, especially the cheeks, appear plump and roly-poly as compared to the all-arms-and-legs look of most twelve-year-olds.

Most characteristic of the six-year-old is his gap-toothed grin! From six to twelve, youngsters lose their baby teeth and acquire most of their permanent ones. As the face is still small, new teeth loom large, so that an eight-year-old, for instance, may sport "tombstone" front teeth. By the time he reaches twelve, the facial growth will have caught up with his teeth.

At six the average child stands slightly over three-and-a-half feet tall; by the time he reaches preadolescence he will be stretching past the five-foot mark. Weight doubles, jumping from an average of 40 pounds to about 80 pounds.

Physical coordination reaches a new peak. At no other time do children have so little fear of the unknown, as in swimming, skating, climbing, or riding.

A striking trait in grade-school children is their declaration of independence.

This results in refusals to take baths, formation of secret clubs, and a desire to do everything on their own. Six-year-olds may occasionally return to babyhood characteristics, such as giggling for no cause or using baby talk. Usually they observe a group and must be encouraged to enter into a game or song. School is new to them so they often require cuddling or tender attention at home before heading out to play or at bedtime.

By the age of nine you'll see few signs of such affection! This is the time for neighborhood clubs or a secret organization. You can win a lasting place in the nine-year-old's heart if you suggest a good place for a clubhouse, then forget that you know where it is.

Eleven- and twelve-year-olds are fiercely independent. They scorn babyish toys or games. Physically and mentally they can take on responsible jobs. This age is nearing adolescence, and extra attention, time, and care must be used to understand changing emotions and needs.

All children share the desire to collect people, ideas, and objects.

All through grade-school years, notice the tendency of youngsters to join in groups, whether it be a noisy clan walking to school or the small, quiet group meeting secretly in a clubhouse.

Does it seem every time you visit John or Tammy you admire a new array of rocks or leaves or sea shells? This, too, follows form, for youngsters love to hoard rocks, sea shells, coins, or model ships and cars. They also delight in interesting contortions like crossing their eyes, or rubbing their stomachs while patting their heads.

You have a head start on understanding this age group if you sometimes hold your breath while crossing a bridge, avoid stepping on cracks in the sidewalk, or catch yourself chanting, "Rain, rain, go away," for you haven't lost the feel of the magic carpet of childhood under your feet.

MOM, COULD YOU GET JOANIE TO SIT FOR ME TONIGHT? SHE PROMISED SHE'D TEACH ME THE LATIN HUSTLE!
LASKY

GOO-GOO! GA-GA! COOTCHIE COOTCHIE COO!
OUR NEW SITTER ISN'T BAD, BUT SHE'S NOT THE MOST INTERESTING CONVERSATIONALIST...

F·O·U·R

Sitter's Guide to Safety

Your first, last, and always concern in babysitting should be for the safety of the child you're with. That's why you're there. If children were capable of taking good care of themselves, you'd be out of business.

Few babysitters are ever involved in a real emergency situation. But, in any business, it pays to be prepared for that "it'll never happen to me" incident.

The best way to avoid problems is, of course, to prevent them. Chapter 3 gave you some ideas for keeping children occupied. And as long as they're busy and under your eye, there's little chance that you'll get involved in rescue work.

But just in case the unexpected should happen, be prepared by:

• Knowing where to reach parents and where first-aid supplies are kept.

- Carrying around a "mental first-aid kit"—the knowledge of how to deal with common problems, and the ability, which comes from knowledge, to act calmly in an emergency.

Here is a quick listing of common accidents and suggestions for dealing with them. They occur most often in the age groups under which they are listed, but can, of course, happen to children of any age.

12 TO 15 MONTHS

FIRE—If a child's clothing catches on fire, do not let him run. Wrap him in any heavy material you can find to smother flames (a rug, blanket, etc.). Get him to a hospital.

POISONING — Call a doctor! Give child a drink of warm water or milk. Get child to hospital, taking poison bottle along. Do not try to induce vomiting unless told to do so by the doctor. If your area has a Poison Control Center, they'll instruct you and help you get to a doctor.

CHOKING—Turn child upside down and slap under shoulder blades. If object won't come out call police or rush child to a hospital. Do not give child water or try to remove object with your finger.

TWO YEARS

BURNS—If minor, hold under cold water or put on burn ointment. If severe, call doctor or rush child to hospital, keeping him warm.

FALLS—If a child refuses to eat, vomits, or is very pale after a fall, call the doctor. Cover child and keep him quiet. If child is unconscious, do not shake or slap him.

DROWNING—Learn lifesaving and artificial respiration in an approved course such as that given by the Girl Scouts or Red Cross.

THREE YEARS

CUTS—If minor, wash with soap and water, bandage loosely. If deep with heavy bleeding, apply pressure to wound with thick cloths and call doctor immediately.

AUTOMOBILES — Never leave a child unattended. If child is hit by a car, get help at once. Cover child and stay with him.

SUNBURN — Prevent by oiling skin and keeping child out of sun. For burn, apply ointment and tell child's parents about burn.

FOUR YEARS

OBJECT IN EYE — Bathe eye gently with lukewarm water. If severe pain continues, call parents or doctor. Do not poke in eye or attempt to turn up eyelid.

BROKEN BONES—Make sure child does not move. Phone for parents and doctor. Keep child as comfortable as possible.

NOSEBLEEDS—Apply cold cloths or ice pack to back of neck or forehead. If nose bleeds more than 10 minutes, call parents.

If you do a lot of babysitting, or want to try one of the "grand-scale babysitting" ideas in Chapter 7, it would be wise to enroll in a first-aid course at your local Red Cross Chapter, YWCA, or a school course.

THAT'S RIGHT, MRS. CHAMBURY-- I PUT BILLY TO BED PRECISELY AT 8:00... AND 9:00... AND 9:30...

THE BAD NEWS IS THAT JONATHAN COMPLETELY REFUSED TO OBEY YOUR "NO SKATEBOARDING IN THE LIVING ROOM" RULE. THE **GOOD** NEWS IS THERE'S A SALE ON BEAUTIFUL NEW TIFFANY LAMPS AT FILBERT'S...

F·I·V·E

Building In Good Behavior

You wouldn't expect a person who'd never had a driving lesson to be able to control a car, but many people expect a child who's never been disciplined to have complete control of his behavior.

No child is born bad, but children are born with instincts for exploring and trying out new things. They are like mirrors, reflecting directly or indirectly the feelings and actions of people around them. They soon learn that all people aren't alike and begin to experiment with differents ways of behaving. Children need help in sorting out behavior patterns and learning which are acceptable for them.

You'll probably be involved in this sorting-out process with children you know. Big sisters, aunts, and babysitters all are faced with discipline problems at some time.

What you learn now can also help you in later years, with your own children.

To begin, learn what good discipline is. Respect for himself and others is the happiest and healthiest reason for a child's good behavior. Punishment, according to Dr. Benjamin Spock, is only a substitute emergency method when the regular system of discipline breaks down. Creating the kind of relationship that helps a child behave means remembering these few important guides.

Set reasonable limits. A good guide to follow is that only fair and necessary restrictions are those that prevent a child from endangering himself or others, or infringing on others' rights.

A child needs to express his feelings. Giving vent to angry or hurt feelings at times may be best for the child—as long as others aren't hurt in the process. Punishment without understanding may cause him to hide his feelings inside, where they build up to volcanic proportions. Help him to get rid of them in constructive ways —pounding nails into old boards, batting a ball around, dressing up in old clothes and pretending he's fighting cowboy or a tough, bad pirate.

Create an atmosphere of love and courtesy, and a child will absorb these ideas. Most adults insist that children say "please" and "thank you" to them, but they never think of giving the same courtesy in return. Children are people too.

Treat a child as a reasonable being who can

understand simple, logical explanations. And remember that he learns a lot by example. Teachers in one nursery school were busy elsewhere when Joe, four, and Mary, three-and-a-half, started fighting over a toy. Tommy, also four, stopped the fight and delivered this little lecture (exactly what he had heard teachers say):

Tommy: Joe, you shouldn't have taken Mary's toy. You should ask her if you can play with it. Mary, you shouldn't have hit him. We have to learn to tell how we feel in words, not by hitting.

Avoid the need for punishment by giving a child materials, space, and time for acceptable activities. Mischief often results from idleness and boredom.

When you must scold a child, make him understand that it is his actions you dislike, not the child himself.

Telling a child repeatedly that he is bad, or naughty, or stupid, destroys his self-respect. Say instead, "I still love you, Johnny, but I'm very unhappy about the thing you've just done."

Remember that one reason for discipline is to help a child handle situations that may be beyond his knowledge or ability. So don't give in just because he protests. But do be ready to review restrictions and remove them as a child learns to handle situations for himself.

The best way to help a child behave is to give him a chance. Don't keep reminding him of an incident of misbehavior after it's over. If he's having a temper tantrum, remove objects that he might hurt himself with, then leave the room, and let him kick out his anger.

When he calms down, wipe his face, give him a hug to let him know you still love him, and suggest a quiet game or story that the two of you can enjoy.

You can't stop a fight by throwing a few punches of your own. Coming down to the child's level and screaming out an argument with him won't solve his problem or yours. The job of anyone who takes care of children is to stay calm, hold the line of authority, and be fair. Here are a few common discipline problems and some suggestions for handling them. Remember that the goal is to help the child discipline himself.

Sassiness—This is meant to annoy you or get you angry, so refuse to be upset. Tell the child calmly that you like him, and that you're sorry he doesn't like you at the moment, then leave him alone until he's ready to cooperate.

Fights—Disregard minor arguments. Stop a serious fight and separate the children. Refuse to take sides.

"Bad" language—Ignore it in young children. Usually they don't understand what they are saying. Make it clear to an older child that he can't use such language around you.

Refusing to eat—A child won't starve if he misses one meal. He may be just tired, or excited, or tense. Offer food in a casual, friendly way and if he won't eat, take it away in the same manner and try again later. Repeated refusal should be looked into by a doctor, of course.

Resisting bedtime —Establish a routine for bedtime and follow it. A child is not necessarily misbehaving when he resists going to bed. He may be feeling lonely, or left out of things, or simply too tired to be sleepy. Don't scold him for getting up the first few times. If it happens many times, tell him firmly that he must stay in bed and offer to sit quietly with him until he goes to sleep.

How do these guidelines fit the idea of permissive discipline, which has been a popular term for the past few years? Permissivness has been misconstrued to mean that you permit a child to do whatever he wants—that you never say "no." In the book mentioned earlier *(Teaching Your Child Right from Wrong)*, Mrs. Whyte explains that permissive discipline really is good discipline, "Setting limits appropriate to a child's stage of development, not unreasonably restrictive, but ones he can understand and accept comfortably."

Understanding what good discipline is should help you to live more happily with the children you know, but it won't prevent you from facing the problem of punishment. *Only parents should punish a child*, so your job at this point will involve just reporting discipline problems to them. But you should learn for future use some ideas about what punishment should or should not be.

Never hit a child. This is inexcusable in any situation. An occasional quick slap, a reaction to being provoked, is something most parents can't avoid. But even this is not often necessary in a friendly household, where children absorb ideas of consideration and courtesy. Hitting should be avoided.

Gear punishment to a child's age and level of understanding, and to the disobedience involved. If Jerry ignores the outdoor boundaries his mother has set, she is justified in keeping him indoors for the rest of his playtime. Taking away the trip to the zoo promised him for the next Saturday would be an unfair and unreasonable punishment.

Review the results of punishment. If it makes a child misbehave more, the punishment is wrong.

Good discipline and just punishment are teaching tools. Use them judiciously and remember, once again, you are *only* the babysitter! It is the parents' responsibility to punish or discipline a child. A babysitter's job is temporarily taking over for a parent. If a child is too difficult to babysit for, if you feel the parents' control or ideas of discipline are too different from your own, don't babysit for that child again. It is not your job to punish or teach discipline to someone else's children.

...AND HERE'S A LIST OF EMERGENCY PHONE NUMBERS, VALERIE- THE POLICE DEPARTMENT, THE FIRE DEPARTMENT, PEPPINO'S TAKE-OUT PIZZA PARLOR...
LASKY-

I'M SORRY, DAVEY WILLIAMS, BUT IT'S TIME FOR YOU TO ASK YOUR FRIENDS TO LEAVE AND GET READY FOR BED. NOW... WHICH OF YOU IS DAVEY WILLIAMS?
LASKU-

S·I·X

The Magic of Play

Blonde, four-year-old Julie peeks from under the blanket-draped chairs calling, "Tommy, bring in those groceries at once."

Tommy, struggling in his father's old suit coat, makes a valiant effort, lifts the "groceries" (possibly a bag of blocks), and scoots through the playhouse doorway.

In the kitchen, Heidi, her eyes round with wonder, follows the soap bubbles she has just blown and chants, "I'm a bubble. I feel happy and sparkly inside."

The magic of play is that a child can be anything he wants to be—a grownup in a real world of jobs and home and family, or a happy bubble floating on top of the world.

But what is play? And how does a child benefit from it?

Play is any activity that a child chooses to take part in and that interests, amuses, or satisfies him. It may be dramatic — pretend games and dress-up play—or simple, noisy—pounding or throwing—or quiet, social or solitary.

Play is a child's work.

Julie and Tommy play "house" and for the time the game lasts they are a real mommy and daddy, with real worries over their children, and the real everyday fun and problems. Tomorrow they may play at being a nurse and doctor, firemen, or a barber and beautician. As they play, they're trying on all the careers from which they'll one day choose their own.

Children take their play seriously. You may have laughed as you watched youngsters acting out their parents' roles with such comment as, "Eat your eggs," "Don't forget your umbrella," or "I'll spank." But you probably noticed, too, how grownup and businesslike the children were as they played. They learn from play because they have the imagination to be what they are playing. Heidi didn't say, "I feel like a bubble." She said, "I am a bubble."

Cooperative play provides a child with opportunities to learn what other people are like. He learns the give-and-take necessary to adult life. He discovers, if group play is properly guided, that he can get along with others and still have a personality of his own.

Play is a child's means of discovery, of communication, and of expression.

Play helps a child learn about the world. He discovers how objects are made and what he can do with them, tests the ways he might behave in different situations, and tries out the various roles he might play as an adult.

How else can children learn the feel of a squirmy worm, or the delightful sound of pots and pans banging on the floor? Sand, trees, rocks, grass, animals, and plants provide endless wonder, questions, and experiments. There's a special satisfaction for a child in the discovery that he can dig and dig and still not run out of dirt, that a pile of rocks can be changed into a castle or fortress.

The wonder of discovery makes it easy for children to communicate their feelings. Timmy finds out what it's like to have an attentive audience when he tells about the squirrel he saw feeding her little ones.

His playmates may like the story of the squirrel so much that they'll all become squirrels, hopping around the room and munching on imaginary nuts. Play gives them a chance to express what they've learned about the world and how they feel about it.

Through creative play a child learns concentration and mastery of skills.

How often have you seen Johnny pounding at a nail, filling and refilling a sand bucket, or driving around and around the playground on a tricycle? He soon learns that there is a great satisfaction in knowing how he wants to do something and doing it just that way. He learns, too, that there are different ways of doing things and that he is free to add his own ideas to what others tell him.

While he is learning how to do things, and doing them over and over, a child is adding to his physical strength.

Batting a ball for hours on end not only helps Ned in the next baseball game, but it makes it easier for him to coordinate his eyes and hands in manual school projects and in other sports.

Through play, a child gains confidence in himself and learns to have pride in the things he does on his own. Paint, clay, building blocks, paper, and paste give him a chance to show how he sees the world and to express his feelings about the events in his life.

But all of these benefits are gained from play only if a child can choose his own activity and can engage in it without pressure or interference.

Do children have time to play? Listen in as Mrs. Sanders tries to arrange piano lessons for nine-year-old Johnny:

"I'd be glad to take Johnny, Mrs. Sanders. Would Thursdays at five be convenient for him?"

"I'm afraid his Scout troop meets then. Do you have another time?"

"Mondays at four, then."

"I'm sorry. Monday is band practice day."

"Perhaps you'd better tell me when he's free and I'll see if I can arrange something."

"Well, Tuesdays and Wednesdays are club days at school, and Friday afternoons his baseball team practices. Saturday mornings would be fine, if he can be finished in time to get to dance classes at one. I don't suppose you teach on Sundays...."

Mrs. Sanders would say Johnny has time to play—he takes part in baseball games and club meetings, goes to dances, and has countless other activities.

Johnny Sanders does have many activities, so many, in fact, that he can do none of them well — and in all of them he is expected to be first and best. As a result, he enjoys none of them and feels that he is a failure.

A time for play — real play — can and should be arranged for every child. All that's required is that adults follow a few simple rules:

Try not to plan every minute of a child's day. Like you, he needs some time that's his own.

Make a real effort not to press your own interests on a child. You may love music, while trying to master the piano is sheer torture for him. Let him find his own special interest and help him to develop it.

Take part in a child's activities when you are asked, but resist the urge to direct things. The game may run more smoothly, or the painting be neater, but the child will have lost the satisfaction of saying, "Look what I did!"

Don't be too critical of a child's work or compare it with that done by other children.

When asked to comment on a child's work, try to visualize what he was striving for, and don't judge his results by adult standards.

Every child is creative — and will express and develop his creativity through some type of play. If adults handle a child's playtime with care, creativity will survive to enrich his later life.

Toys: The Tools Of Play

Although play doesn't necessarily involve toys, most children today have an endless collection of things to play with.

As a babysitter, you'll probably be adding to the toy collection of some of the children you get to know well. If you choose wisely, the toys you give can be tools for helping the child enjoy and learn from play.

Toys should be safe, versatile, easily handled, and durable. They must be fun to play with, of course, or the child will ignore them. Most important to the learning process, toys should appeal to the child's imagination and inspire him to adapt them to all kinds of different activities.

One simple way to decide whether a toy is a good one is to ask yourself these questions:

Does the toy fit the child's physical skill? Many toys are discarded or destroyed because they are so simple they bore the child or so complicated that they frustrate him. Watch him as he plays and see what type of toy he can handle. For example, you'll see that most small children can't control their fingers well enough to enjoy a toy with small levers and buttons. These are usually broken off very quickly and often are swallowed.

Will the toy teach the child something? Children find learning fun and like toys that satisfy curiosity. A toy can give a little boy a safe look at the underside of a truck, or let a little girl practice "cook" on safe equipment made for her size.

Is the toy well made? Until muscle control is well-learned, a child can't always be gentle in handling objects. A good toy can take a few bumps. Check to see that seams are tightly glued and projecting parts firmly attached. Toys made of plastic are less likely to shatter into sharp pieces if the label says they're "high impact plastic."

HELLO! THIS IS ANDREW, COMING TO YOU FROM HIS BEDROOM ON OUR NEW HOME VIDEO SURVEILLANCE SYSTEM! WHEN DO I GET MY MILK AND COOKIES?
LASKY-

MARILYN SHOULD BE ABLE TO HANDLE OUR KENNY QUITE WELL, DEAR-- I UNDERSTAND SHE USED TO TRAIN THE CHIMPS AT THE CITY ZOO!
LASKY

S·E·V·E·N

About Books for Children

Lisa, age four, can tell you a lot about her world, and one of the reasons is that someone has taught her to love books.

A love of books is not an instinctive thing, natural to all children. Children do have a curiosity about the world, which includes books if they are part of that world. But a child who truly loves books, who loves to read or to be read to, has *learned* to do so — from his parents, from babysitters, from all kinds of pleasant everyday experiences with books.

You can help a child you know to have this same good feeling about books—a feeling that will help him in school years when reading ability can affect his achievements in all areas.

Try these suggestions, from *What's Best for Your Child and You*, by Dr. David Goodman (Association Press):

Buy books. A well-stocked library lends distinction to a home and encourages reading.

Books for children can be picked up at department stores, in book stores, through book clubs, but they shouldn't be just picked up. You wouldn't go to a shelf marked "books for teenagers" and grab the book closest to you. A child's book should be selected as you'd select something you want to read — considering reading ability, interests, and needs at that particular time. Choice of any book, says Mary Eakin, *Good Books for Children* (University of Chicago Press), can be made on the basis of these three standards:

Literary quality: Characters should be realistic, plot logically developed. Nonfiction material should be presented in a straightforward, factual way.

Quality of content: Books should have substance. Social and ethical standards should be observed. For example, national, racial, or religious groups should be treated realistically and with tolerance for individual characteristics. Family and other relationships should be sound and healthy.

Suitability of style and content: The writing style and physical format of a book should be geared to a child's level of development. Complex plots and characters are best reserved for older children. Large illustrations and type appeal to young readers.

If you're new at selecting children's books, begin with a good list. The *Horn Book Magazine* is an excellent guide to children's books and reading, and publishers often supply age-graded lists.

Once you've learned a little about what's available, try to rely less on age charts. Observe a child's reactions to books for his age level. If he seems bored, provide some "older" ones. Try out any book you think he'll like, even if tradition calls it too simple or too advanced for him.

Use these guidelines for choosing books for a child, but make sure they apply to the child you know:

Look for action in the first two or three paragraphs. Most children like fast starts.

Find books that have a variety of words and sounds.

Let a child help in choosing his own books. Introduce him to the library and book store.

When the child is about three, take him to the public library to participate in the "picture book hour," which most libraries now offer for little children.

Begin establishing the library habit by having him take home picture books. Make a festive date of going to the library with him every two weeks or so until it becomes a regular habit and he goes willingly without other inducement.

Cultivate the delightful pastime of reading aloud to a child. This is good preparation for his later reading. The read-to child nearly always becomes a good reader.

Choosing a book may be easier for you than the actual reading or telling of a story. If so, remember these few points:

Read a story until you know it. You can then watch the child's reactions without losing your train of thought.

Learn to add drama to a story. Facial and vocal expressions tell a child clearly what the words mean.

If a child asks you to read the same story again, do it. He may need the security of the familiar.

Realize that there will be times when the story reading or telling will be unsuccessful. Respect the child's right to choose his own recreation and stop your reading.

When the child starts school, quietly observe his first steps in learning to read. Beware of showing anxiety, but at the same time, if he doesn't seem to master it try to find out why. It is very difficult to recover from a bad start in reading.

Discuss books at mealtimes. Good table talk is a great stimulus to the intellectual development of a child.

Your attitude about books and reading will be an important influence on any child who knows you.

Try, when you spend time with children, to give them enjoyable experiences with books. If you carry toys or treats with you, take along one or two favorite children's books. If a child asks you to read a story, do so willingly and with pleasure. Practice reading children's stories, using facial and vocal expressions to make them "come alive." Most of all read and appreciate good books whenever you can.

Here are a few of the best-loved books for

children. Try them on the youngsters you know. *Goodnight Moon*, Margaret Wise Brown (Harper & Row), or *The Three Billy Goats Gruff*, Asbjornsen and Moe (Harcourt, Brace), for small children; *Horton Hatches the Egg*, Dr. Seuss (Random House), or *Mike Mulligan and His Steam Shovel*, Virginia Lee Burton (Houghton Mifflin), for four-and five-year-olds; *The Five Chinese Brothers*, Claire Bishop (Coward, McCann & Geoghegan), or *Clifford, The Big Red Dog*, Norman Bridwell (Four Winds Press), six- to eight-year-olds; *The Borrowers*, Mary Norton (Harcourt, Brace), or *The Wind in the Willows*, Kenneth Grahame (Scribner), nine- to twelve-year-olds.

Unlike Alice's tardy friend, the White Rabbit, you're just in time — to start the children you know on an exciting journey through the wonderland of books.

BUT MY P.J.'S DON'T MATCH -- THE TOPS ARE WINNIE THE POOH, AND THE BOTTOMS ARE DARTH VADER!

BILLY, YOU DON'T HAVE TO GO TO BED AT EIGHT TONIGHT.. AS A MATTER OF FACT, YOU CAN PLAY ALL NIGHT LONG!
1
THAT'S GREAT! THANKS A LOT!
2
SO MUCH FOR REVERSE PSYCHOLOGY...
CASKU-
3

E·I·G·H·T

Babysitting as Big Business

If your venture into the babysitting business is as successful as we expect it to be, you may want to think about branching out.

There are all kinds of avenues open for girls who have had babysitting experience. You might get a part-time job as a nurse's aid in a hospital children's ward, or spend summers counseling at camps.

If you'd rather be your own boss, you can turn your simple babysitting service into a more organized "big business."

Here are three ways you can become a "grand scale" babysitter. Your town may offer other possibilities so be alert for ways you can put your talent and experience to work.

Summer Jobs With Children

As a babysitter you may have an edge on most of your friends in the summer job scramble.

Why? Because you have some job experience to offer an employer. And most towns offer some kind of summer job that involves children.

If there's a park and playground near you, find out whether they have a recreation program for children. If they do, chances are they hire extra help in the summer.

Check with local service organizations (Red Cross, YWCA, YMCA) for job openings with their children's swimming classes or clubs.

Find out whether there are any children's camps near you. They'll have jobs for counselors, waitresses, sports instructors, etc. And you'll have time off to enjoy camp life.

Ask the public library about their children's story hour program — they may need extra help in the summer.

Don't forget that your regular babysitting customers can be your best source of job information. They'll be up on what your town has to offer for children and may be able to give you job leads.

A Babysitting Service

If you've been professional and dependable about babysitting you probably are getting more calls than you can handle alone.

You can keep your customers calling and make extra money by starting a babysitting service. Here's how:

Hold a meeting with the most reliable, capable people you know who are interested in sitting (preferably people from different neighborhoods) and explain your plan to them.

Suggest that each person read our hints for babysitters and encourage discussion. You'll want to be sure that your sitters have the know-how to handle the various situations they are sure to encounter. Monthly meetings will help solve any difficulties they may experience.

Have each sitter compile a list of all the families with children that she or he knows and send out neatly typed postcards announcing your service to each. If you like, illustrate the card with some simple, amusing sketch. Perhaps your announcement will read like this:

THE SITTERS FOUR

ANNOUNCE A NEW BABYSITTING SERVICE
AFTERNOONS, EVENINGS, AND WEEKENDS
TO SECURE OUR SERVICES, PLEASE CALL:
JENNY BROWN, SECRETARY, 17 PINE ST. ME 6-7712
TELEPHONE BETWEEN 4 AND 5 AND 7 AND 8

WE CHARGE ___¢ AN HOUR (TIME AND A HALF
AFTER MIDNIGHT) FOR CONSCIENTIOUS,
EXPERIENCED CARE OF YOUR CHILDREN.

As secretary, you should receive something for your bookkeeping and telephone duties. You may wish to ask your employees for a small percentage of each babysitting fee or you may decide to charge each sitter a fixed rate on joining your organization. You should keep a large notebook in which you record each sitter's name, address, phone number, age, and definite times when she or he is available for sitting. Sometimes a sitter may feel she or he can do best with children in a certain age group. Jot that down and take it into consideration when pairing sitters with parents.

After your sitters sit for the first time, enter their experience with the children in a separate section of your notebook. Comment on number, ages, and names of children and their general behavior; whether the parents arrived home on time; whether transportation home for the sitter was arranged; whether the sitter was expected to do any cleaning up aside from regular sitting duties.

If one of the children presented a particular problem—such as bedwetting or reluctance to eat—make a note of it so that a new sitter will know what to expect from her job.

Of course, if possible, it's best to assign the same sitter to the same children. However, when a mother does not ask for the same person again, it is reasonable to assume that her services were not particularly suited to the situation.

Summer Nursery School

If your babysitting talents can survive the test of taking care of more than one child at a time, you may want to follow the lead of a New Jersey teenager and organize a summer play school.

"The most important suggestion I can give," says Cheryl Jeromin, 17, "is that you learn not to be too bossy. Children will try hard not to obey if you act like a power-happy dictator. Ask for their suggestions and opinions; treat them like people."

Other guidelines, whether you care for a large group or only two or three children, are:

Make definite plans ahead of time. Children need some kind of structure in group activities and will be hard to handle without it. Have an opening activity, one or two things to bring them together during playtime, and a closing activity.

Be flexible. If you've planned an art period around animals and the children are all excited about the latest moon shot, save your idea for another day. Children are usually interested in what goes on around them, so keep up on community activities and encourage them to do the same.

Be businesslike. Let children know in the beginning that there are rules to follow and that you expect their obedience and cooperation.

Get to know each child as quickly as possible and recognize individuality. Cheryl and her assistant planned free periods each day when the children could choose their own activities. Songtime and a chance for each child to tell about his family's vacation encouraged individuality.

Plan special group projects. Children will learn cooperation by working with others. Cheryl's nursery school students helped her plan their parade around the neighborhood and participated in an art show put on for mothers. A play, puppet show, creative dance, etc., would give all the children a chance to work together.

Use your talents. Perhaps you're a good storyteller, or the type who can get others enthusiastic about games. Children love simple tricks — such as knowing how to fold a handkerchief into animal shapes — so don't count any talent too small.

Recognize your responsibility. Safety is something you can't leave to luck. Make sure that the play area is free of things that invite accidents — broken glass, rusty nails, garden tools, machinery — and that barriers block the way to driveways and streets. See that climbing equipment is sturdy. Let children make a safety inspection with you at the beginning of each day's session. Be sure you know basic first aid.

Here are some practical suggestions for organizing your nursery school.

Your schoolhouse. An ideal place to hold your play school is on a school playground where playground equipment and toilet facilities are available. Or perhaps your community has a public park where those facilities would be available, too. You may wish to hold your school in your own backyard and use your basement for rainy-day quarters.

Get some lightweight cartons in which you can store and easily move supplies. You'll need art materials, such as clay, paper, paints, crayons, coloring books, paint brushes, jars for water, blunt scissors, old magazines, and paste. You'll also want story and picture books (ask children to bring some from home, purchase a few, and borrow some from the library), pillows, dolls, blocks, and small toys. Carry fresh or canned juices, crackers, napkins, and paper cups separately, keeping fresh juice in an insulated container. The tuition you decide to charge for your pupils should cover the cost of these items and net you a fair profit.

Your pupils. It's wise to enroll children who live in your neighborhood to eliminate transportation problems. Limit your group to about five children unless you want to get an assistant. Since you will want to plan a program which appeals to all your students, you must decide on a certain age group and admit only those children.

You will, of course, check with parents in regard to any unusual characteristics their child may have. You may find that one of your pupils still has lapses in his toilet training; that one child is allergic to orange juice; or that another tires easily. While you should always be on the alert and prepared to handle each child's differences, you'll also want to relax and enjoy your summer undertaking. So be prepared ahead of time for these small problems.

Your equipment. In order to charge a fair tuition rate, you must decide on the equipment you'll need and the financial outlay you'll have to make for it. You should have a large thermos for juice, plus napkins, paper cups, cans of fruit juice, and cookies.

You'll also need a first-aid kit.

Stock up on colored paper, blunt-edged scissors, paste, crayons, clay, and any other creative play materials you choose. Since children love to dig, you should purchase some inexpensive pails and shovels.

Look for play materials around your own home: empty egg cartons and frozen-juice cans, boxes of all sizes, soda bottle caps, empty thread spools, toothpicks, straws, and macaroni products in different shapes which can be strung on dental floss.

You'll want to estimate the cost of food for special occasions, such as a Fourth of July or a birthday celebration. On these special days, invite the children to lunch and serve a simple soup-and-sandwich lunch with a pretty dessert —a sure hit with any child.

Buy a "registration book" where you can enter parents' names, addresses, and phone numbers and keep an attendance record for each child.

If you have an assistant, you'll have to take her salary into consideration, too.

When you've determined approximately how much money you'll have to pay out, you can decide on a tuition figure which will cover your expenses and allow you to make a fair profit.

Your curriculum. You may choose to hold school in the morning or afternoon, but limit your sessions to a maximum of three hours since young children soon become restless.

The whole glorious outdoors can serve your program well, for children are fascinated by nature and infinitely curious about worms, flowers, tadpoles, rocks. They will delight in nature walks, an afternoon at the community swimming pool, a picnic, a special children's movie, a trip to the fire station, amusement park, zoo, post office, local dairy, etc. Often, parents will be glad to help with transportation. Your library has innumerable books which will prepare you to answer your pupils' questions (and there will be many).

Vigorous outdoor play on playground equipment or active outdoor games (again your library will offer a fund of suggestions) and trips to various interesting places will be only one part of your curriculum. Plan a half-hour story period every day. Select books with bright pictures and try to preface a trip by reading to the children about the place you'll be visiting.

You'll want to divide your sessions into periods; an active play period when children are first deposited with you, then a quiet play period. Schedule a rest period next, then another active play period and, finally, a quiet period before the children go home.

Though you may plan each period for half an hour, it's best to change activities when the children show signs of restlessness or lack of interest. Small children don't have the ability to stick to one activity for long.

At midsession, serve your pupils a small

glass of juice or milk with a cracker or cookie. Refreshments should be followed by the 15-minute rest period when the children stretch out on blankets and listen to a story. Small fries need rest even when they don't think so, so insist on this.

Your daily schedule. You may arrange to have the children brought to your home or to wherever the school is being held. When it is time for them to leave, have them help you put away materials. See that each child is picked up by parents. Then use your next hour or so to plan the next day's activities. After that, you're free for relaxation.

As Cheryl Jeromin did with her "Kiddie Scouts," you'll find that caring for a group of children can be as easy as watching one or two. And the fun, and money, multiply for any teenager who goes in for babysitting on a grand scale!

NOW LET ME GET THIS STRAIGHT-- CINDERELLA SPLITS HER PAD AND HEADS OFF TO THIS DISCO...
LASICU.

NOW TELL A BEDTIME STORY FOR FLUFFY, AND ONE FOR CLOWNY, AND ONE FOR BUDDY...
LASKU-

N·I·N·E

What Every Babysitter Should Know

What would you say if a prospective customer for your babysitting services were to take it into her head to ask you a few questions about your handling of children? Would you panic — or rattle off the answers with assurance? Take the quiz right now and find out. The correct answers are on page 78. Pat yourself on the back if you get at least eight answers right, because you know your business. (The review didn't hurt, though, did it?) If you should happen to do poorly, however, study the answers. Apply them each time you babysit.

Review our sitting tips in Chapters 1 through 7. Remember that when you're employed as a sitter, you not only make much-needed cash, but you're preparing yourself to be a responsible adult and future parent. Better babysitting to you!

QUIZ

1. As his mother and father leave the house, Johnny cries to go with them. Should you:

    ____a. let his mother handle him?
    ____b. spank him?
    ____c. try to divert his attention?

2. Johnny would like to have you read to him. Would you:

    ____a. select a book you believe he would enjoy?
    ____b. let him select a book?
    ____c. suggest another type of entertainment?

3. Johnny scatters toys all over the house. Should you:

    ____a. pick up the toys yourself?
    ____b. make a game of putting the toys away?
    ____c. suggest he pick up the toys himself, but don't make an issue of it?

4. Johnny wants to watch television, but his sister Jane doesn't want to. Would you suggest:

    ____a. another type program?
    ____b. that you and she take this opportunity to do something else while he watches TV?
    ____c. turning the television off?

5. You prepare a bedtime snack. Johnny spills his milk. Would you:

   ____a. have him mop it up?
   ____b. leave it for his mother?
   ____c. have him help you mop it up and assure him that minor accidents happen to everyone?

6. A neighbor drops by and asks if she may leave her children with you while she and her husband go out. Would you:

   ____a. agreeably say it's okay?
   ____b. ask for additional fees?
   ____c. refuse flatly but politely, saying that when you were asked to sit, no mention was made of keeping her children?

7. A child you're sitting with suddenly develops a stomach ache. Would you:

   ____a. call the child's mother and ask for instructions?
   ____b. call the doctor?
   ____c. give the child an aspirin?

8. A child you're taking care of doesn't want to go to bed. Would you:

   ____a. make him a bed on the couch?
   ____b. be firm about time for bed, but tell him stories to induce him to go?
   ____c. insist on the announced bedtime and whisk him off to bed without preliminaries?

9. Once the children are in bed, your employer will appreciate you most if you:

   ____a. collapse on the sofa to recover.
   ____b. try to make the house as neat as you found it.
   ____c. take this opportunity to visit on the telephone with friends.

QUIZ ANSWERS

1. c; 2. b; 3. b; 4. b; 5. c; 6. c; 7. a; 8. b; 9. b.

IN ACCORDANCE WITH OUR CONTRACT, I, DANNY JACOBSON, AGREE TO BEHAVE MYSELF ON THE CONDITION THAT I GET A CHOCOLATE ICE CREAM SUNDAE BEFORE BEDTIME. IN ADDITION, I AM GRANTED A SPECIAL OPTION OF STRAWBERRY OR ALMOND NUT TOPPING...
LASKY-

WHAT A FRUSTRATING EVENING, PATTY! THERE'S NOTHING IN THE REFRIGERATOR, IT TOOK ME AN HOUR TO GET SHELDON TO SLEEP, AND "MORK AND MINDY" WAS PRE-EMPTED!
LASKY

IT WAS A CINCH GETTING BILLY TO SLEEP, MRS. STONE! I JUST TOLD HIM IT WAS "TRANSCENDENTAL MEDITATION"!

IT'S A REAL BUMMER BABYSITTING FOR THE WOLLNERS, DIANE! THEY'RE VEGETARIANS, AND ALL I CAN DIG UP TO EAT IS SPINACH AND BEAN SPROUTS!
LASICH

For My Information

PHONE NUMBERS:

Parents_____

Relative_____

Neighbor_____

Doctor_____

Fire Department — Dial Operator and ask for Fire Department.

Police — Dial Operator, ask for police.

EQUIPMENT:

Diapers, bedclothes, blankets_____

_____

First-Aid Kit _____

INSTRUCTIONS FOR FEEDING:

Time _____

Menu and where to find food_____

_____

Range (how to light) _____

INSTRUCTIONS FOR BEDTIME:

Time _____ Bath_____

Snack _____ Ventilation _____

TIME PARENTS ARE EXPECTED BACK

_____

For My Information

PHONE NUMBERS:

Parents_____

Relative_____

Neighbor_____

Doctor_____

Fire Department — Dial Operator and ask for Fire Department.

Police — Dial Operator, ask for police.

EQUIPMENT:

Diapers, bedclothes, blankets_____

_____

First-Aid Kit _____

INSTRUCTIONS FOR FEEDING:

Time _____

Menu and where to find food_____

_____

Range (how to light) _____

INSTRUCTIONS FOR BEDTIME:

Time _____ Bath_____

Snack _____ Ventilation _____

TIME PARENTS ARE EXPECTED BACK

_____

For My Information

PHONE NUMBERS:

Parents_____

Relative_____

Neighbor_____

Doctor_____

Fire Department — Dial Operator and ask for Fire Department.

Police — Dial Operator, ask for police.

EQUIPMENT:

Diapers, bedclothes, blankets_____

_____

First-Aid Kit _____

INSTRUCTIONS FOR FEEDING:

Time _____

Menu and where to find food_____

_____

Range (how to light) _____

INSTRUCTIONS FOR BEDTIME:

Time _____ Bath_____

Snack _____ Ventilation _____

TIME PARENTS ARE EXPECTED BACK

_____

For My Information

PHONE NUMBERS:

Parents_____

Relative_____

Neighbor_____

Doctor_____

Fire Department — Dial Operator and ask for Fire Department.

Police — Dial Operator, ask for police.

EQUIPMENT:

Diapers, bedclothes, blankets_____
_____

First-Aid Kit _____

INSTRUCTIONS FOR FEEDING:

Time _____

Menu and where to find food_____
_____

Range (how to light) _____

INSTRUCTIONS FOR BEDTIME:

Time _____ Bath_____

Snack _____ Ventilation _____

TIME PARENTS ARE EXPECTED BACK
_____

For My Information

PHONE NUMBERS:

Parents_____

Relative_____

Neighbor_____

Doctor_____

Fire Department — Dial Operator and ask for Fire Department.

Police — Dial Operator, ask for police.

EQUIPMENT:

Diapers, bedclothes, blankets_____

_____

First-Aid Kit _____

INSTRUCTIONS FOR FEEDING:

Time _____

Menu and where to find food_____

_____

Range (how to light) _____

INSTRUCTIONS FOR BEDTIME:

Time _____ Bath_____

Snack _____ Ventilation _____

TIME PARENTS ARE EXPECTED BACK

_____

For My Information

PHONE NUMBERS:

Parents_____

Relative_____

Neighbor_____

Doctor_____

Fire Department — Dial Operator and ask for Fire Department.

Police — Dial Operator, ask for police.

EQUIPMENT:

Diapers, bedclothes, blankets_____

_____

First-Aid Kit _____

INSTRUCTIONS FOR FEEDING:

Time _____

Menu and where to find food_____

_____

Range (how to light) _____

INSTRUCTIONS FOR BEDTIME:

Time _____ Bath_____

Snack _____ Ventilation _____

TIME PARENTS ARE EXPECTED BACK

_____

For My Information

PHONE NUMBERS:

Parents_____

Relative_____

Neighbor_____

Doctor_____

Fire Department — Dial Operator and ask for Fire Department.

Police — Dial Operator, ask for police.

EQUIPMENT:

Diapers, bedclothes, blankets_____
_____

First-Aid Kit _____

INSTRUCTIONS FOR FEEDING:

Time _____

Menu and where to find food_____
_____

Range (how to light) _____

INSTRUCTIONS FOR BEDTIME:

Time _____ Bath_____

Snack _____ Ventilation _____

TIME PARENTS ARE EXPECTED BACK

_____